Why Christmas?

The Christmas Edition of *Why Jesus?*

Nicky Gumbel

Illustrated by
Charlie
Mackesy

Expanded

Alpha

Published by Alpha International,
HTB Brompton Road, London, SW7 1JA.

Email: internationalpublishing@alpha.org
Website: alpha.org
@alphacourse

Illustrations by Charlie Mackesy

Why Christmas?

Why celebrate Christmas?

There is something almost magical about Christmas: children dream of Father Christmas and his fantasy sleigh, we picture Christmas trees, snowy scenes, filled-up stockings, piles of presents and smiling families around the fire in matching knitted Christmas jumpers.

The reality is often not as perfect as we imagine. Some people go way over the top. The overcrowding on the streets and in the shops can lead to so-called 'Santa-Claustrophobia'.

Over-indulging takes its toll on family life. One nine-year-old boy wrote, 'I know Christmas should be a religious time, but to me Christmas is a time for the necessities of life such as food, presents and booze.' As American satirist P. J. O'Rourke mused, 'There is a remarkable breakdown of taste and intelligence at Christmastime. Mature, responsible grown men wear neckties made of holly leaves and drink alcoholic beverages with raw egg yolks and cottage cheese in them.'

For some, there is a danger of over-spending – buying presents that others do not need with money they have not got.

One little girl wrote to her granny, 'Thank you very much for the nice gloves you sent me for Christmas. They were something I wanted – but not very much!'

Others can become over-demanding. One doting father asked his small daughter well in advance what she would like for Christmas. Shyly she announced she would like a baby brother. To everyone's surprise and delight her mother returned from hospital on Christmas Eve with a baby boy in her arms. When the father repeated the question next year, there was less hesitation. 'If it wouldn't be too uncomfortable for Mummy, I would like a pony!'

But while some go over the top, others struggle. For many, Christmas is one of the worst times of the year. For some it's the loneliest time of year. Suicide rates go up, more people die from 'natural causes', marriages fall apart, psychiatrists' patients suffer regressions and family feuds begin.

One Mori poll suggested that there are three million family rows each Christmas. One newspaper article spoke of people breaking down at Christmas as a result of the pressure to be perfect. According to the mental health charity Mind, at least one in ten people struggle to cope with the pressure of having the 'perfect Christmas' and suffer as a result.[1] Another article reported that two psychologists, a psychotherapist and a counsellor were running a workshop entitled 'Stress in the family: coping with Christmas'. They said that part of its success seemed to be the chance it offered to get away from it all. The psychiatrist, Anthony Storr, in an article on depression at Christmas entitled, 'Cheer up, it's soon over' had this final piece of advice: 'Remember that Christmas, although recurrent, doesn't last for ever.'

With all the magic, the stress and the hype of Christmas, are we missing the point? What is at the heart of Christmas? In the words of C. S. Lewis, at Christmas we remember the 'central event in the history of the earth – the very thing the whole story has been about'.

Why bother with Jesus?

When Jesus was born a group of highly intelligent philosophers thought he was worth bothering with. They stopped everything to take him three symbolic presents. The first was gold – a present fit for a king. The child in the manger was the King of kings and Lord of lords. God himself had come to live as part of our world. Too often Jesus has been obscured by Christmas. One man wrote to *The Times:* 'Sir: Failing to find any religious books in the bookshop, I asked an assistant for help.

She showed me an inconspicuous handful of Bibles and prayer books, saying: "We have had to move them down to the bottom shelf because of Christmas."'

But the point of Christmas is Jesus Christ. At Christmas we celebrate the birthday of the most important person who has ever lived. He is the centrepiece of our civilisation. After all, we call what happened before his birth 'BC' and what happened after 'AD'.

But how do we know it is true?

We can test the claims of Christianity because it is an historical faith. It is based on the life, death and resurrection of Jesus Christ. Our faith is based on firm historical evidence.

Who is Jesus?

Jesus was and is the Son of God. Some people think he was just a 'good religious teacher'. However, that suggestion does not fit with the facts.

a) His claims

Jesus claimed to be the unique Son of God – on an equal footing with God. He assumed the authority to forgive sins. He said that one day he would judge the world and that what would matter then would be how we had responded to him in this life.
C. S. Lewis pointed out: 'A man who was merely a man and said the sort of things Jesus said would not be a great moral teacher.' He would either be insane or else he would be 'the Devil of Hell'. 'You must make your choice,' he writes. Either Jesus was, and is, the Son of God or else he was insane or evil but, C. S. Lewis goes on, 'let us not come up with any patronising nonsense about his being a great human teacher. He has not left that open to us. He did not intend to.'[2]

b) His character

Many people who do not profess to be Christians regard Jesus as the supreme example of a selfless life. In an interview, Albert Einstein said, 'I am enthralled by the luminous figure of the Nazarene. Jesus is too colossal for the pen of phrase-mongers, however artful.' He further added: 'No man can read the Gospels without feeling the actual presence of Jesus. His personality pulsates in every word. No myth is filled with such life.'[3] As far as his teaching is concerned, there seems to be general agreement that it is the purest and best ever to have fallen from human lips.

As C. S. Lewis put it, 'It seems obvious that he was neither a lunatic nor a fiend; and consequently, however strange or terrifying or unlikely it may seem, I have to accept the view that he was and is God. God has landed on this enemy occupied world in human form.'[4]

c) His conquest of death

The evidence for the physical resurrection is very strong indeed. When the disciples went to the tomb they found that the grave clothes had collapsed and that Jesus' body was absent.

In the next six weeks he was seen by over 500 people. The disciples' lives were transformed and the Christian Church was born, and then grew at a dynamic rate.

A former Lord Chief Justice of England, Lord Darling, said of the resurrection: 'In its favour as living truth there exists such overwhelming evidence, positive and negative, factual and circumstantial, that no intelligent jury in the world could fail to bring in a verdict that the resurrection story is true.' The only satisfactory explanation for these facts is that Jesus did indeed rise from the dead and thus confirms that he was, and is, the Son of God.

The wise men were right. Nothing less than gold would be suitable for such a child.

Why do we need him?

Even if Jesus was who he said he was, why do we need him 2,000 years later? The second gift the wise men brought was frankincense, which was used in the temple as the symbol of prayer and pointed to a relationship with God.

Relationships are exciting. They are the most important aspect of our lives – our relationships with our parents, boyfriend or girlfriend, husband or wife, children, grandchildren, friends, and so on.

Christianity is first and fore-most about relationships rather than rules. It

is about a Person more than a philosophy. It is about the most important relationship of all: our relationship with the God who made us. Jesus said that the first and greatest commandment is to love God. The second is to love our neighbour. So, it is also about our relationships with other people.

You and I were created to live in a relationship with God.

Until we find that relationship there will always be something missing in our lives. As a result, we are often aware of a gap. One rock singer described it by saying: 'I've got an emptiness deep inside.'

One woman, in a letter to me, wrote of 'a deep, deep void'. Another spoke of 'a chunk missing in her soul'.

People try to fill this emptiness in various ways. Some try to close the gap with money, but that does not satisfy. Aristotle Onassis, who was one of the richest men in the world, said at the end of his life: 'Millions do not always add up to what a man needs out of life.'

Others try drugs or excess alcohol or sexual promiscuity. One woman said to me, 'These things provide instant gratification but they leave you feeling hollow afterwards.' Still others try hard work, music, sport or seek success. There may not be

anything wrong with these in themselves but they do not satisfy that hunger deep inside every human being.

Even the closest human relationships, wonderful though they are, do not in themselves satisfy this 'emptiness deep inside'.

12

Nothing will fill this gap except the relationship with God for which we were made.

According to the New Testament, the reason for this emptiness is that men and women have turned their backs on God.

Jesus said, 'I am the bread of life' (John 6:35). He is the only one who can satisfy our deepest hunger because he is the one who makes it possible for our relationship with God to be restored.

a) He satisfies our hunger for meaning and purpose in life

At some point everyone asks the question, 'What am I doing on earth?' or, 'What is the point of life?' or, 'Is there any purpose to life?' As the French philosopher Albert Camus once said, 'Man cannot live without meaning.'

Until we are living in a relationship with God we will never find the true meaning and purpose of life. Other things may provide passing satisfaction but it does not last. Only in a relationship with our Creator do we find the true meaning and purpose of our lives.

b) He satisfies our hunger for life beyond death

Before I was a Christian I did not like to think about the subject of death. My own death seemed a long way in the future. I did not know what would happen and I did not want to think about it. I was failing to face up to reality. The fact is that we will all die.

Yet God has 'set eternity in the human heart' (Ecclesiastes 3:11). Most people do not want to die. We long to survive beyond death. Only in Jesus Christ do we find eternal life. For our relationship with God, which starts now, survives death and goes on into eternity.

c) He satisfies our hunger for forgiveness

If we are honest, we would have to admit that we all do things that we know are wrong. Sometimes we do things of which we are deeply ashamed. More than that, there is a self-centredness about our lives which spoils them. Jesus said, 'What comes out of you is what makes you "unclean". For from within, out of your hearts, come evil thoughts, sexual immorality, theft, murder, adultery, greed, malice, deceit, lewdness, envy, slander, arrogance and folly. All these evils come from inside and make you "unclean"' (Mark 7:20–23).

Our greatest need, in fact, is for forgiveness. Just as someone who has a serious illness needs a doctor whether they realise it or not, so we need forgiveness whether we realise it or not. Those who recognise their need are far better off than those who are lulled into a false sense of security.

By his death on the cross Jesus made it possible for us to be forgiven and brought back into a relationship with God. At Christmas we remember the fact that Jesus entered our world in order to restore relationships – first our relationship with God and then our relationships with others. In this way he supplied the answer to our deepest need.

Why did he come?

Why did Jesus come? How could he achieve this restoration of our relationship with God? The third present the wise men brought gives us the answer. Myrrh was used to embalm the bodies of the dead. Jesus is the only man who has ever chosen to be born and he is one of the few who has chosen to die. He said that the entire reason for his coming was to die for us. He came 'to give his life as a ransom for many' (Mark 10:45). The supreme reason for giving Christmas presents is to remind us of his gift to us – the most valuable and expensive gift ever given.

From what we know of crucifixion it was one of the cruellest forms of execution. Cicero (106-43 BC) described it as 'the most cruel and hideous of tortures'. Jesus would have been flogged with a whip of several strands of leather weighted with pieces of metal and bones. According to Eusebius, a third-century historian, 'The sufferer's veins were laid bare, and the very muscles, sinews and bowels of the victim were opened to exposure.' Jesus was then forced to carry a six-foot cross beam until he collapsed.

When he reached the site of execution, six-inch nails were hammered through his wrists and feet as he was nailed to the cross. He was left to hang for hours in excruciating pain. Yet, the New Testament makes it clear that there was something worse for Jesus than the physical and emotional pain; this was the spiritual anguish of being separated from God as he carried all our sins.

Why did he die?

Jesus said he died 'for' us. The word 'for' means 'instead of'. He did it because he loved us and did not want us to have to pay the penalty for all the things that we had done wrong. On the cross he was effectively saying, 'I will take all those things on myself.'

He did it for you and he did it for me. If you or I had been the only person in the world he would have done it for us. St Paul wrote of 'the Son of God, who loved me and gave himself for me' (Galatians 2:20). It was out of love for us that he gave his life as a ransom.

The word 'ransom' comes from the slave market. A kind person might buy a slave and set him free – but first the ransom price had to be paid. Jesus paid, by his blood on the cross, the ransom price to set us free.

Freedom from what?

a) Freedom from guilt

Whether we feel guilty or not, we are all guilty before God because of the many times we have broken his laws in thought, word and deed. Just as when someone commits a crime there is a penalty to be paid, so there is a penalty for breaking God's law. 'The wages of sin is death' (Romans 6:23).

The result of the things we do wrong is spiritual death – being cut off from God eternally. We all deserve to suffer that penalty. On the cross Jesus took the penalty in our place so that we could be totally forgiven and our guilt could be taken away.

b) Freedom from addiction

Jesus said that 'everyone who sins is a slave to sin' (John 8:34). Jesus died to set us free from that slavery. On the cross, the power of this addiction was broken. Although we may still fall from time to time, the power of this addiction is broken when Jesus sets us free. That is why Jesus went on to say that 'if the Son sets you free you will be free indeed' (John 8:36).

c) Freedom from fear

Jesus came so that 'by his death he might destroy him who holds the power of death – that is, the devil – and free those who all their lives were held in slavery by their fear of death' (Hebrews 2:14–15).

We need no longer fear death. Death is not the end for those whom Jesus has set free. Rather it is the gateway to heaven, where we will be free from even the presence of sin. When Jesus set us free from the fear of death, he also set us free from all other fears.

Freedom for what?

Jesus is no longer physically on earth but he has not left us alone. He has sent his Holy Spirit to be with us. When his Spirit comes to live within us, he gives us a new freedom.

a) Freedom to know God

The things which we do wrong cause a barrier between us and God: 'Your iniquities have separated you from your God' (Isaiah 59:2). When Jesus died on the cross he removed the barrier that existed between us and God. As a result he has made it possible for us to have a relationship with our Creator. We become his children.

The Spirit assures us of this relationship and he helps us to get to know God better. He helps us to pray and to understand God's word (the Bible).

b) Freedom to love

'We love because he first loved us' (1 John 4:19). As we look at the cross we understand God's love for us. When the Spirit of God comes to live within us we experience that love. As we do so we receive a new love for God and for other people. We are set free to live a life of love – a life centred around loving and serving Jesus and loving and serving other people rather than a life centred around ourselves.

c) Freedom to change

People sometimes say, 'You are what you are. You can't change.' The good news is that with the help of the Spirit we can change. The Holy Spirit gives us the freedom to live the sort of lives that deep down we have always wanted to live. St Paul tells us that the fruit of the Spirit is 'love, joy, peace, patience, kindness, goodness, faithfulness, gentleness and self-control' (Galatians 5:22–23).

When we ask the Spirit of God to come and live within us, these wonderful characteristics begin to grow in our lives.

Why not?

In Christ Jesus, God offers us forgiveness, freedom and his Spirit to live within us. All this is a gift from God. When someone offers us a present we have a choice. We can either accept it, open it and enjoy it. Or else we can say, 'No thank you.' Sadly, many people make excuses for not accepting the gift which God offers.

Here are some of the excuses:

a) 'I have no need of God'

When people say this they usually mean that they are quite happy without God. What they fail to realise is that our greatest need is not 'happiness' but 'forgiveness'. It takes a very proud person to say that they have no need of forgiveness.

We all need forgiveness. Without it we are in serious trouble. For God is not only our loving Father; he is also a righteous judge. Either we accept what Jesus has done for us on the cross, or else one day we will pay the just penalty ourselves for the things we have done wrong.

b) 'There is too much to give up'

Sometimes, God puts his finger on something in our lives which we know is wrong and which we would have to give up if we want to enjoy this relationship with God through Jesus.

But we need to remember:

- God loves us. He asks us only to give up things which do us harm. If I saw some small children playing with a carving knife I would tell them to stop, not because I want to ruin their fun but because I do not want them to get hurt.

- What we give up is nothing compared to what we receive. The cost of not becoming a Christian is far greater than the cost of becoming a Christian.

• What we give up is nothing compared to what Jesus gave up when he died on the cross for us.

c) 'There must be a trap'

Understandably, people often find it hard to accept that there is anything free in this life. They think it all sounds too easy and that there must be some hidden trap. However, what they fail to realise is that although it is free for us, it was not free for Jesus. He paid for it with his own blood. It is easy for us, but it was not easy for him.

d) 'I'm not good enough'

None of us is good enough. Nor can we ever make ourselves good enough for God. But that is why Jesus came. He made it possible for God to accept us just as we are, whatever we have done and however much of a mess we have made of our lives.

e) 'I could never keep it up'

We are right to think that we could never keep it up. We cannot by ourselves, but the Spirit of God, who comes to live within us, gives us the power and the strength to keep going as Christians.

f) 'I'll do it later'

This is perhaps the most common excuse.

Sometimes people say, 'I know it's true but I'm not ready.' They put it off. The longer we put it off the harder it becomes and the more we miss out. We never know whether we will get another opportunity. Speaking for myself, my only regret is that I did not accept the gift earlier.

What do we have to do?

The New Testament makes it clear that we have to do something to accept the gift that God offers. This is an act of faith. St John writes that 'God so loved the world that he gave his one and only Son that whoever believes in him shall not perish but have eternal life' (John 3:16). Believing involves an act of faith, based on all that we know about Jesus. It is not blind faith. It is putting our trust in a Person. In some ways it is like the step of faith taken by a bride or a bridegroom when they say, 'I will' on their wedding day.

The way people take this step of faith varies enormously but I want to describe one way in which you can take this step of faith right now. It can be summarised by three very simple words:

a) 'Sorry'

You have to ask God to forgive you for all the things you have done wrong and turn from everything which you know is wrong in your life. This is what the Bible means by 'repentance'.

b) 'Thank you'

We believe that Jesus died for us on the cross. You need to thank him for dying for you and for the offer of his free gift of forgiveness, freedom and his Spirit.

c) 'Please'

God never forces his way into our lives. You need to accept his gift and invite him to come and live within you by his Spirit. If you would like to have a relationship with God and you are ready to say these three things, then here is a very simple prayer which you can pray and which will be the start of that relationship:

Lord Jesus Christ,

I am sorry for the things I have done wrong in my life (take a few moments to ask his forgiveness for anything particular that is on your conscience). Please forgive me. I now turn from everything which I know is wrong.

Thank you that you died on the cross for me so that I could be forgiven and set free.

Thank you that you offer me forgiveness and the gift of your Spirit. I now receive that gift.

Please come into my life by your Holy Spirit to be with me forever.

Thank you, Lord Jesus. Amen.

What now?

1. Tell someone

It is important to tell someone in order to underline the decision you have made. Often it is only when you tell someone else that it becomes a reality to you. It is probably best to start by telling someone who you think will be pleased to hear the news.

2. Read the Bible

Once we have received Jesus and put our trust in him we become children of God. He is our heavenly Father. Like any father he wants us to have a close relationship with him.

We develop this relationship as we listen to him (primarily through the Bible) and as we speak to him in prayer. The Bible is the word of God and you might find it helpful to begin by reading a few verses of John's Gospel every day. Ask God to speak to you as you read.

3. Start to speak to God each day (ie pray)

I find the following a great help:

A – Adoration
Praising God for who he is and what he has done.

C – Confession

Asking God's forgiveness for anything that we have done wrong.

T – Thanksgiving

Thanking God for health, family, friends and so on.

S – Supplication

Praying for ourselves, for our friends and for others.

4. Join a lively church

It is important to be part of a group of Christians who get together to worship God, to hear what God is saying to them, to encourage one another and to make friends. Church should be an exciting place!

I first prayed a prayer like the one on page 24 on 16 February, 1974. It changed my life. It is the best and most important thing I have ever done. I trust it will be the same for you.

Further reading:

Questions of Life by Nicky Gumbel, which looks in greater detail at the relevance of Jesus to our lives today and explores the basics of the Christian faith.

30 Days by Nicky Gumbel, is a practical introduction to reading the Bible. Whether you've been a Christian for years, but find reading Scripture a struggle, or you're exploring faith for the first time, *30 Days* will help you start reading the Bible in an easy and accessible way.

Go Deeper

Bible in One Year is a free daily Bible reading resource with notes provided by Nicky and Pippa Gumbel as they take you through every chapter and verse of the Bible, sharing their thoughts and prayers. Each day includes a passage from the Old Testament, a Psalm or Proverb and a passage from the New Testament so, in the course of one year, you can read the whole Bible.

Intended to be read or listened to alongside the Bible to provide fresh understanding of the texts, the *Bible in One Year* app can be downloaded for free from the App Store or on Google Play. You can also listen to the *Bible in One Year* on your favourite podcast player, subscribe to the daily emails at bibleinoneyear.org or purchase the book from **shop.alpha.org.**

The following pages are selected excerpts from the *Bible in One Year.*

bibleinoneyear.org

Your Key to Life

• Madonna said, 'When I was growing up... Jesus Christ was like a movie star, my favourite idol of all.'[5]

• Napoleon Bonaparte said, 'I know men and I tell you that Jesus Christ is no mere man.'[6]

• Novelist H.G. Wells said, 'I am an historian, I am not a believer. But this *penniless preacher* from Galilee is irresistibly the centre of history.'[7]

Even people who would not describe themselves as followers of the 'penniless preacher' recognise that there is something extraordinary about Jesus.

No one, not even angels, can compare to Jesus (Hebrews 1:1–14). If you want to know what God is like, look at Jesus. He said, 'Anyone who has seen me has seen the Father' (John 14:9). Everything you read and understand about God through the Bible needs to be read through the lens of Jesus. He is the ultimate revelation of God.

Your key to getting your life sorted out is Jesus. Your key to understanding the Bible is Jesus. Your key to understanding God's character is Jesus. Your key to life is Jesus.

Psalm 119:129–136
Jesus provides cleansing from our sins

Reading the Bible is, in some ways, like looking in a mirror with a very bright light: 'The unfolding of your words gives light' (v.130a). The light reveals what is wrong with our life and what we need to have cleaned up. It reveals the things that cause a barrier between us and God.

This barrier was removed when Jesus provided cleansing for your sins. Through Jesus, you can be confident that God's face will shine upon you (v.135).

Pray like the psalmist:
'Turn to me and have mercy on me,
    as you always do to those who love
        your name.
Direct my footsteps according to
        your word;
    let no sin rule over me.
Redeem me from human
        oppression,
    that I may obey your precepts.
Make your face shine upon your
        servant' (vv.132–135a).

The psalmist's prayer foreshadows the great act of Jesus in providing purification for sins. Through Jesus always turn to God with confidence knowing that he will have mercy, 'as you always do to those who love your name' (v.132).

Prayer

Lord, thank you for Jesus. Thank you for your mercy. May no sin rule over me. Keep me from pride, anger, lust, greed, envy, prayerlessness, rivalry and all the other temptations of life. I pray that you would make your face shine upon me today.

NEW TESTAMENT READING

Hebrews 1:1–14
Jesus is superior to angels

Jesus is unique and he is all you need. As Eugene Peterson points out, you do not need Jesus-and-angels. You do not need Jesus-and-Moses. You do not need Jesus-and-priesthood. 'This letter deletes the hyphens, the add-ons.' *All you need is Jesus.*

The book of Hebrews is all about who Jesus is and how he is better and greater than any other being, teaching, or religious system. It opens with a comparison between Jesus and the Old Testament prophets. It explains the wonderful truth of how God spoke through the prophets, but then describes how Jesus is *even better* (vv.1–3). He is 'the heir of all things', he was involved in creation, he is the ultimate revelation of God, he is your sustainer, and he is your redeemer. The reason for all of this lies in who Jesus is.

Jesus 'is the radiance of God's glory and the exact representation of his being' (v.3). As *The Message* puts it, he 'perfectly mirrors God, and is stamped with God's nature.'

Jesus came to sort out our lives. 'After he had provided purification for sins, he sat down at the right hand of the Majesty in heaven' (v.3b). Sitting down symbolises the fact that his work was finished (see also John 19:30).

There have always been people who can't accept this truth. Today, some argue that Jesus was 'just a great religious teacher', and nothing more. In a similar way, at the time of this letter, some people were arguing that Jesus was 'just an angel'. The writer of Hebrews says: 'So he became as much superior to the angels as the name he has inherited is superior to theirs' (Hebrews 1:4). He then goes on to argue the superiority of Jesus over the angels.

There are nearly 300 references to angels in the Bible. What do we know about them?

In this passage we see that angels worship and serve God (vv.6–7). They are God's messengers (v.7, MSG). They are spiritual beings who serve Christians (v.14). They 'are sent to serve those who will inherit salvation' (v.14).

Angels are nearer than you think. They guard and protect you. God has given 'his angels charge of you to guard you in all your ways' (Psalm 91:11). For example, an angel strengthened Jesus at Gethsemane (Luke 22:43). Each church has one (Revelation chapters 1–3).

But Jesus is far greater. The writer of Hebrews sets out seven passages from Old Testament Scriptures to show the superiority of Jesus over the angels (Psalm 2:7; 2 Samuel 7:14; Deuteronomy 32:43; Psalms 45:6–7; 102:25–27; 104:4; 110:1).

All these passages are the answer to anyone who says that Jesus was only an angel or (more likely today) a 'great religious teacher'. The peak of the argument is in Hebrews 1:8, 'About *the Son* he says, "Your throne, O *God..."'* This is an outright ascription of *divinity to Jesus.* Jesus is the one whose identity is God.

Prayer
Lord, thank you that you send angels to guard and protect us. Thank you that they serve us. But thank you even more for Jesus, who is far superior to all angels.

OLD TESTAMENT READING
....

Lamentations 3:40–5:22
Jesus is the anointed Messiah

The writer of Lamentations says, 'Let us lift up our hearts and our hands' (3:41). The lifting of hearts and hands seem to go together in prayer. Raising hands in prayer is not eccentric or weird, it is the traditional form of prayer in both the Old Testament and New Testament.

The writer calls the people to pray and says, 'Let's take a good look at the way we're living and reorder our lives under God' (v.40, MSG). This is an important discipline in a life of faith. Ask God to reveal if there are any areas of your life that you need to change.

If there are, then return to God in confession and repentance (v.42 onwards). Now you know that you will be forgiven and your relationship with God will be restored because of what Jesus has done for you. This passage, like so many others in the Old Testament, points forward to Jesus.

The writer of Lamentations says, 'You, O Lord, reign f*or ever; your throne* endures from generation to generation' (5:19).

The writer of Hebrews says of Jesus: '"*Your throne,* O God, will last for ever... therefore God, your God, has set you above your companions by *anointing you* with the oil of joy"' (Hebrews 1:8–9). Jesus is God's anointed one – the Christ, the Messiah.

He is the one to whom all the Scriptures point. The people of God were expecting the Lord's anointed. The writer of Lamentations speaks of '*the Lord's anointed*' (Lamentations 4:20). The Hebrew word for anointed one is 'Meshiach' from which we get the word Messiah. He goes on to say, 'to you also the cup will be passed' (v.21). Jesus spoke of the cup he would drink (Mark 10:38; John 18:11). Jesus was alluding to the cup of God's wrath against sin.

God's anger is not like ours. It contains no element of spite, pettiness or hypocrisy. It is the reaction of a holy and loving God towards sin. Passages like this help us to understand how serious our sin is in God's sight and how amazing it is that, on the cross, Jesus bore the wrath of God for you and me.

The prophet sees that they are cut off from God by their sin: 'You have covered yourself with a cloud so that no prayer can get through' (Lamentations 3:44). This is the barrier that Jesus removed when he drank the cup of God's wrath and provided purification for sins. This is the answer to the prayer of the writer of Lamentations when he prayed, 'Restore us to yourself, O Lord, that we may return; renew our days as of old' (5:21).

Because of Jesus, the Anointed One and the one who drank the cup, God's presence is no longer covered with a cloud, and your prayers can get through to him. You can lift up your heart and your hands to God. He will restore you and renew you.

Although there are many words about judgment in the Bible, they can be read through the lens of Jesus who revealed the true character of God and provided purification for your sins.

Prayer
Father, thank you for Jesus. Thank you that I can know and understand who you are through Jesus. Thank you that the key to life is in Jesus.

Pippa Adds
Hebrews 1:7,14
'In speaking of the angels he says, "[God] makes his angels winds, his servants flames of fire"' (v.7).

'Are not all angels ministering spirits sent to serve

those who will inherit salvation?' (v.14).

I have heard of unexplainable stories of rescue or remarkable intervention that may well have been an angel. It is hugely encouraging to know there are angels descending from heaven, flying around helping those who are in desperate need of God.

Why Christmas?

Today we celebrate the 'central event in the history of the earth, the very thing the whole story has been about'[8] (C.S. Lewis). We celebrate the birth of Jesus. It is a day of great joy and celebration around the world.

And yet, in the midst of all the trappings and celebrations of Christmas, it can be easy to miss *why* Jesus' birth is so significant. The key to Christmas lies, not in the details of the shepherds' visit or the wise men's journey, but in the identity of the one whom they came to worship. In Jesus, God became 'flesh' and 'made his dwelling among us' (John 1:14). Christmas is about Jesus!

Our New Testament passage for today helps us to grasp something of the magnitude of what that means. In it we are reminded that 'baby Jesus' is also the 'Lord of lords and King of kings'

(Revelation 17:14b). We are given a glimpse of the cosmic struggle between good and evil, as a vast array of powers and authorities line up against God. Yet we are reminded that, in the end, it is through the humility and self-sacrifice of 'the Lamb' that they are overcome.

Jesus puts aside the glories of heaven for a humble stall. As the carol, *Hark! The Herald Angels Sing*, puts it:

Christ, by highest heaven adored;
Christ, the everlasting Lord;
late in time behold him come,
offspring of a virgin's womb.
Veiled in flesh the Godhead see;
hail the incarnate Deity,
pleased as man with man to dwell,
Jesus, our Emmanuel.
Hark! The herald angels sing,
'Glory to the new born King!'[9]

In each of today's passages we see the blessings of following this 'new born King'.

OLD TESTAMENT READING

Psalm 147:12–20
Blessing, peace and satisfaction

All the promises of God were fulfilled when Jesus came. God promised his people blessing, peace and satisfaction ('the best bread on your tables', v.14, MSG). He 'launches his promises earthward' (v.15, MSG).

When the birth of Jesus was announced to shepherds, the angel described it as 'good news of great joy for all the people' (Luke 2:10). The heavenly hosts praise God for 'peace on earth' (v.14). Jesus had been born in Bethlehem (meaning 'the house of bread'). He is the one who satisfies the spiritual hunger in the heart of every human being.

Prayer

Lord, thank you for the way in which you bless your people. Thank you that 'we have peace with God through our Lord Jesus Christ' (Romans 5:1). Thank you that you satisfy the deepest longings of my heart.

NEW TESTAMENT READING
....

Revelation 17:1–18
Called, chosen and faithful

Christmas is not only a nice story, but a decisive moment in human history. In the cosmic battle between good and evil, God and the devil, Jesus is the decisive figure. That battle, and Jesus' centrality and victory in it, is the focus of our New Testament passage for today.

Sometimes, the church appears to be fighting a losing battle. In Western Europe today, church attendance has been in decline for some time. Secularism *appears* to be winning. The book of

Revelation reveals what is happening behind the scenes, and how things will ultimately turn out.

As we look around at our world, it is immensely powerful, attractive and seductive at one level. Yet, beneath the surface we see so much evil and so much opposition to the Lamb.

The opposition to Jesus is personified in 'Babylon the Great, the mother of prostitutes and of the abominations of the earth' (v.5), which is written on the woman who rides on a beast.

In the original context, the identity of 'Babylon' is ancient Rome. As we have seen, the 'seven hills on which the woman sits' (v.9) are the seven hills around Rome.

Superficially, there was something very attractive about the Roman Empire, representing all that the world offers. She is 'dressed in purple and scarlet, and was glittering with gold, precious stones and pearls' (v.4).

But beneath the superficial attraction lay violence and vice: 'With her the kings of the earth committed adultery and the inhabitants of the earth were intoxicated with the wine of her adulteries' (v.2).

It gradually becomes apparent that despite appearances to the contrary, this violence and vice was not random, but specifically targeted against God and his people. The array of characters that appear in the first half of the passage 'have one purpose... they will make war against the Lamb' (vv.13–14).

The wonderful news of this passage is that

the Lamb wins. He doesn't only win, but he also includes you in his victory: 'They will make war against the Lamb, but the Lamb will overcome them because he is Lord of lords and King of kings – and with him will be his *called, chosen* and *faithful* followers' (v.14). As the church often comes under great attack and the forces of darkness sometimes seem to be in the ascendency, I find this verse to be a great comfort and encouragement.

As Mother Teresa said, 'God does not call me to be successful; he calls me to be *faithful*.' If you are faithful to Jesus you will ultimately be successful, because Jesus will ultimately succeed.

Celebrate today the privilege of being one of those *called, chosen* and *faithful* followers of Jesus. Jesus, the baby, born that first Christmas day, grew up, died as the Lamb of God and was raised to life.

Ultimately the Lamb will overcome all evil 'because he is Lord of lords and King of kings' (v.14). That is wonderful news to celebrate this Christmas. As one of the great Christian carols puts it, we have a saviour 'to free all those who trust in Him from Satan's power and might. O tidings of comfort and joy!'

Prayer

Lord, thank you that you are Lord of lords and King of kings. Thank you that you rule and reign. Thank you that ultimately the Lamb will overcome all the forces of evil. Help me to stick close to Jesus and be among his faithful followers.

Nehemiah 3:1–4:23
Rebuilding, restoring and repairing

Christmas day especially, is a day when, all over the world, the name of Jesus should be honoured. Sadly, it is so often not the case. What can you contribute to seeing the name of Jesus honoured in our world?

Jerusalem was the city of God where God dwelt. God had called Nehemiah and the people to rebuild the walls of Jerusalem. This is a wonderful visual illustration of the task of the church today. We are called to rebuild and repair so that the name of Jesus may be honoured again in our society.

Do you ever wonder 'Am I needed?'; 'Do I have anything to offer?'; 'Is what I do of any value or significance?'.

In this passage, we see that *everyone* was needed. *Everyone* went to work shoulder to shoulder, side by side, rebuilding, restoring and repairing. Each was given a portion of different lengths. The key is not to compare, but simply to get on with whatever God calls you to do.

God notices what you do and values what you do. 2,500 years later, we are still reading what the people of God did here. Their names are listed.

They were all volunteers. None of them appear to have been professional builders by trade. They were businesspeople, entrepreneurs, rulers, nobles, goldsmiths and perfume-makers. Yet they were willing to offer themselves for the task of rebuilding. All ages were involved (3:12).

They might have been tempted to think that what they were doing did not seem very significant. Malkijah the ruler was asked to repair the *Dung* Gate! He did not complain that it was beneath him. He simply got on with it. Together they were part of something very significant. They were rebuilding Jerusalem. They were bringing honour to God's name.

Opposition and ridicule came from the outside (4:1–8) and discouragement from within (vv.10,12). The same was true for Jesus. His birth was not welcomed by all. Herod tried to kill him. The opposition to Jesus and his church continues today.

You do not need to be afraid (v.14). Through a combination of prayer and action, success is possible. When opposition comes, respond like Nehemiah (v.9) with increased prayer and extra vigilance. They never dropped their guard (v.23).

The key: 'Our God will fight for us!' (v.10). With God fighting for us, a nation can be changed, churches can be filled, family life strengthened, marriage honoured, the crime rate can fall and society can be transformed. Most important of all, the name of Jesus can be honoured again.

As you look around at the state of the church, get involved in this task of rebuilding. Be willing to work hard and not to be put off by opposition.

Prayer

Lord, thank you that the Lamb always wins – that the one whose birth we celebrate today will ultimately be victorious because he is 'King of kings and Lord of lords'.

Pippa Adds

Psalm 147:14 says, 'He grants peace...' Or, as it says in Isaiah, 'He will be called Wonderful Counsellor, Mighty God, Everlasting Father, Prince of Peace. Of the increase of his government and peace there will be no end' (Isaiah 9:6–7a).

Peace is what is needed this Christmas: peace in our hearts, peace in the world, peace everywhere.

Notes:

[1] Annie Corcoran, *Independent*, 'Why the pressure for the perfect Christmas is bad for our mental health', Wednesday 26 December 2018.

[2] *Mere Christianity* by CS Lewis © CS Lewis Pte Ltd 1942, 1943, 1944, 1952.

[3] 'What Life Means to Einstein: An Interview by George Sylvester Viereck,' *The Saturday Evening Post*, 26 October 1929, p.17. www.saturdayeveningpost.com/wp-content/uploads/satevepost/what_life_means_to_einstein.pdf

[4] *Mere Christianity* by CS Lewis © CS Lewis Pte Ltd 1942, 1943, 1944, 1952.

[5] Robert P. Vande Kappelle, *Truth Revealed: The Message of the Gospel of John — Then and Now* (WIPF & STOCK, 2014), p.xii.

[6] Madonna, SPIN, May 1985.

[7] Josh McDowell, *Evidence That Demands a Verdict* (Here's Life Publishers, San Bernardino, 1986), p.127.

[8] C.S. Lewis, *Joyful Christian* (MacMillan Publishing Company, 1984) p.53.

[9] Charles Wesley, 'Hark the Herald Angels Sing'.

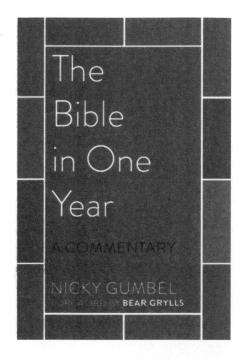

The Bible in One Year: A Commentary by
Nicky Gumbel published by Hodder & Stoughton,
is available to purchase from **shop.alpha.org**

ISBN 978-1-47367-706-7 (Hardback)
ISBN 978-1-47367-707-4 (Paperback)

Try Alpha

Alpha is a series of interactive sessions that explore the Christian faith.

Alpha

Each talk looks at a different question around life, faith and meaning, and is designed to spark discussion.

Alpha runs in cafés, churches, homes, and even online. Each session has three key elements: a time to connect, a talk, and space for good conversation.

Find out more about Alpha at:
alpha.org.uk

To purchase Alpha resources, head to:
shop.alpha.org